Word by Word Graded Readers

Book 1

KEY WORDS
FLASH CARDS

Look

Look at Kim.

good

Kim is good.

am

I am a good boy.

Philip Gibson

Read aloud the words and sentences below.

Hello.

Lee

Hello, Lee.

Pat

Hello, Pat.

and

Lee and Pat.

Pat and Lee.

Kim

Hello, Kim.

Lee, Pat and Kim.

like / likes

Lee likes Pat.

Pat likes Lee.

Lee likes Kim.

Lee likes Pat and Kim.

I

I like Lee.

I like Pat.

I like Lee and Pat.

too

I like
Kim, too.

good

is

Lee is good.

Pat is
good, too.

Pat is good and
Lee is good, too.

Look

Look.
Pat is good.

at

Look at Kim.
Kim is good.

Look at Lee.
Lee is good, too.

a

boy

Lee is a boy.

Lee is a good boy.

girl

Look at Pat.

Pat is a girl.

Pat is a good girl.

here

Look. Look here.

Kim is here.

Look at Kim.

dog

Kim is a dog.

Kim is good.

Kim is a
good dog.

Look. Look here.
A boy, a girl
and a dog.

A good boy,
a good girl
and a good dog.

am

I am a boy.

I am a
good boy.

I am good and
Pat is good, too.

I am a good boy,
and Pat is a
good girl.

Pat is good and
I am good, too.

Yes

Is Pat here?
Yes. Pat is here.

Kim is
here, too.

No.

Is Lee a girl?
No. Lee is a boy.

Is Pat a boy?
No. Pat is a girl.
Pat is a good girl.

Hello.
Look.

Lee is here and
Pat is here, too.

Here is Pat and
here is Lee.
Kim is here, too.

Lee is a good boy,
and Pat is a good girl.

Kim is a good dog.

I like Lee, Pat
and Kim.

Note for parents and teachers

If the young reader can read and understand all the above words and sentences, he/she will be able to easily read and understand the story in the first Word by Word graded reader:

Lee and Pat

See the book on Amazon here:
http://amzn.to/1Nh0M3Q

Happy Reading!

Word by Word Graded Readers

Book
2

KEY WORDS
FLASH CARDS

This is Pat.

This is Lee.

Look at the ball.
The ball is big.

banana

orange

This is an apple.

Philip Gibson

Practice reading aloud the key words and sentences below.

He / he

Look at Lee.
He is good.
He is a good boy.

She / she

You can write the words and sentences here.

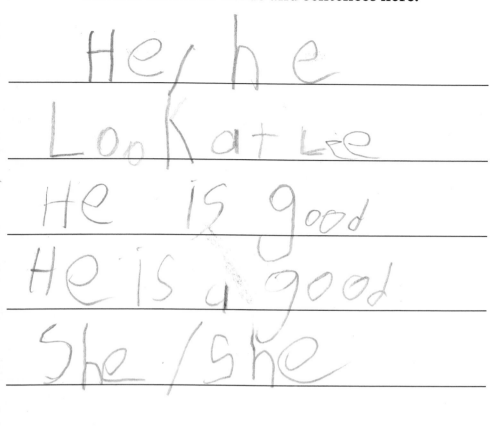

He he

Look at Lie

He is good

He is a good

She she

Look at Pat.
She is good.
She is a good girl.

with

Pat is with Lee.

You can write the words and sentences here.

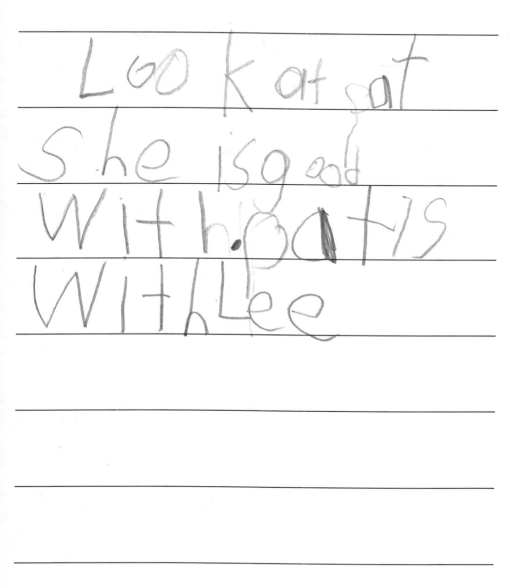

Look at cat
she is good
with bat is
with lee

Lee is with Pat.

play / plays

Lee plays with Pat. He plays with Kim, too.

You can write the words and sentences here.

Lee is N pat
play s play
Lee play With
pat. He play With Kim too.

33

Look at Kim.
Kim plays with
Lee and Pat.

not

Is Lee here?
No. Lee is
not here.

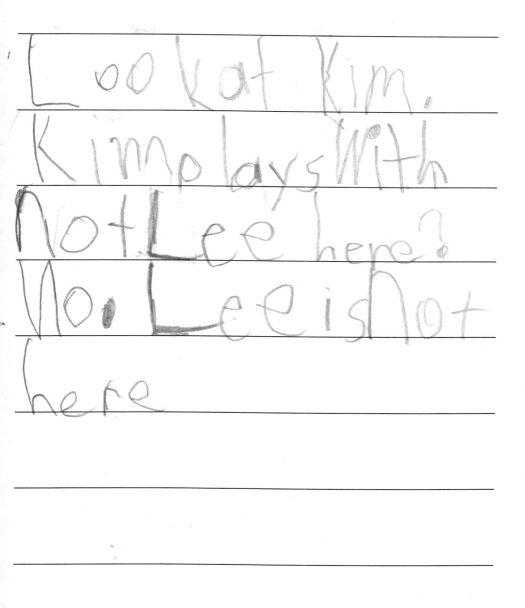

Look at Kim.
Kim plays with
Not Lee here?
No. Lee is not
here

Is Pat here?
Yes. Pat is here.
Lee is not here.

Pat is here. She
is here with Kim.
Lee is not here.

to

You can write the words and sentences here.

Is pa there?

yes, pa t is here

Pat likes to play. She likes to play with Kim.

Lee likes to play with Pat. He likes to play with Kim, too.

This

You can write the words and sentences here.

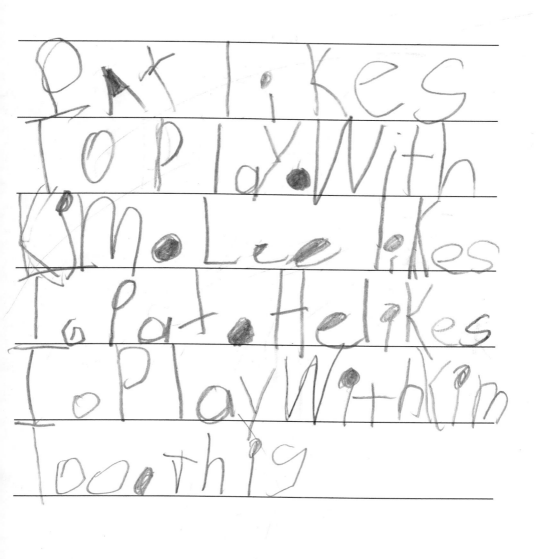

Pat likes
To play with
Kim. Lee likes
To Pat. He likes
To play with Kim
too this

This is Lee.

This is Pat.

an apple

You can write the words and sentences here.

This is Lee

This is Pat

a apple

This is an apple.

ball

It / it

You can write the words and sentences here.

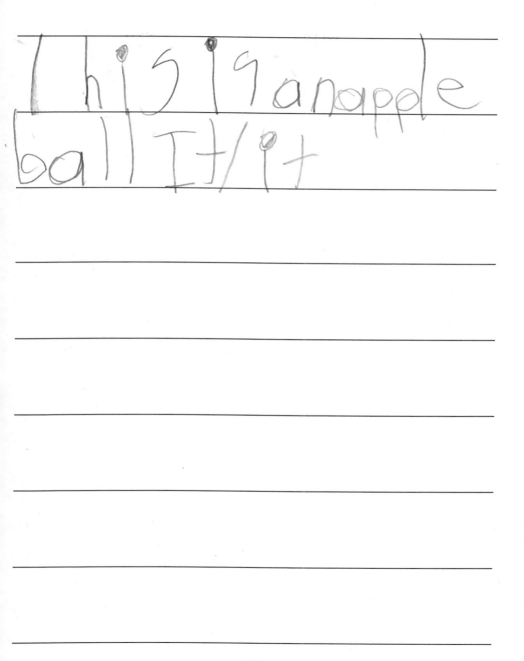

This is a apple
ball It/It

Is this an apple?
No, it is not. It is
not an apple. It is a ball.

Is this a ball?
No, it is not. It is
not a ball. It is an apple.

big

You can write the words and sentences here.

Is this an apple

No, it is not

It is

Look at this ball.
It is big. It is
a big ball.

Pat likes the big ball.
She likes to play
with this big ball.

The / the

You can write the words and sentences here.

Look at the ball.
The ball is big.

Pat and Kim play
with the big ball.

They / they

You can write the words and sentences here.

Pat and Kim like to play.
They like to play
with the big ball.

Pat and Kim like the big ball.
Lee likes this apple.
He likes the big apple.

banana

You can write the words and sentences here.

Look at the banana
and the apple.

book

Pat likes books.
Lee likes bananas.

You can write the words and sentences here.

orange

Lee likes oranges, too.

ice-cream

You can write the words and sentences here.

Lee likes
bananas, oranges
and ice-creams.

has

Lee has an
ice-cream. He has
an orange, too.

You can write the words and sentences here.

Pat has a book.
Pat likes books.

Pat's book is not small.
It is big.
It is a big book.

Are / are

You can write the words and sentences here.

Look.
Are they apples?
No, they are not.
They are oranges.

Look.
Is it a big book?
No, it is not.
It is a small book.

You can write the words and sentences here.

Lee and Pat are
here. They are
here with Kim.
They like to play. They like
to play with Kim, the dog.

Look at the books.
They are big books.
Lee and Pat like
the big books.

You can write the words and sentences here.

Pat likes big books.
Big books are good.
Pat has the big book.
She likes this book.

Lee has a book, too.
He has a small book.
Small books are good, too.

You can write the words and sentences here.

Goodbye

Goodbye, Lee.
Goodbye, Pat.

Goodbye, Kim.

Goodbye.

You can write the words and sentences here.

Note for parents and teachers

If the young reader can read and understand all the above words and sentences, he/she will be able to easily read and understand the story in the second Word by Word graded reader:

Lee and Pat like to play

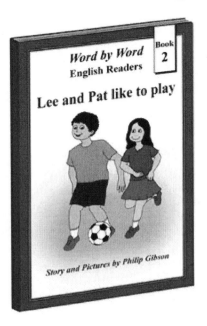

See the book on Amazon here:
http://amzn.to/1QAcTwZ

Happy Reading!

Word by Word Graded Readers

Book
3

KEY WORDS
FLASH CARDS

teacher

The dog likes me.

Kim is in
the garden.

Tree / tree

Mommy

Look at the tree.
The cat is in the tree.

Philip Gibson

teacher

Look at the teacher. He is a very good teacher.

Does / does

You can write the words and sentences here.

Does the
teacher like Pat?
Yes, he does.

Does the teacher like Lee,
too? Yes, he does. The
teacher likes Lee, too.

Look at Kim. Does Kim
like the ball?
Yes, he does.

You can write the words and sentences here.

House / house

Look at this house.
It is not a small house.
It is big. It is a big house.

Does Lee like this house?

Yes, he does.

You can write the words and sentences here.

cat

Here is a cat.
This cat is not big.
It is a small cat.

That / that

You can write the words and sentences here.

Pat likes that cat.
Lee does not.
Lee does not like that cat.

In / in

The cat is
in the house.
Lee does not like that.

You can write the words and sentences here.

You / you

You are a good girl, Pat.

You like books.

Garden / garden

You can write the words and sentences here.

This is a garden.

Kim is in
the garden.

Lee and Pat are
in the garden, too.

You can write the words and sentences here.

or

Is this Lee or Pat?
This is Pat.

Happy / happy

You can write the words and sentences here.

Pat is happy. She is in the house with the cat.

The cat is happy, too. The cat likes Pat.

Very / very

You can write the words and sentences here.

Pat is good.
She is very good.
She is a very good girl.

want / wants

Pat wants to play.
She wants to play
with the cat.

You can write the words and sentences here.

Fun / fun

It is fun to play.
It is fun to play
with the cat.

Where... ?

You can write the words and sentences here.

Where is Lee?
Lee is in
the garden.

Where is Pat?
Pat is in the house.

Tree / tree

You can write the words and sentences here.

Look at the tree.
The cat is in the tree.

Go / go

That cat likes
to go in the tree.

You can write the words and sentences here.

It's / it's

Is it a big tree?
Yes, it's very big.
It's a very big tree.

Can / can

You can write the words and sentences here.

Can the cat go in
the tree? Yes, it can.
It can go in the tree.
It can not go in the house.

Water / water

The cat does not go
in water. The cat
does not like to go in water.

You can write the words and sentences here.

over there

Look over there.
The cat is over
there in the tree.

Lee's dog.

You can write the words and sentences here.

Pat's cat.

Lee's dog is in the house.

Pat's cat is not in the house. Pat's cat is in the tree.

You can write the words and sentences here.

Do / do

Do you like Pat's cat?

Yes, I do.

Daddy

You can write the words and sentences here.

Daddy likes
Pat's cat, too.

Lee does not
like Pat's cat.

Car / car

You can write the words and sentences here.

Lee's dog can
go in the car.

Pat's cat can not
go in the car.

me

You can write the words and sentences here.

The dog likes me.

Come / come

The dog can come with me.

You can write the words and sentences here.

Don't / don't

I don't want the cat
to come in the house.
I don't like that cat.

Mommy

You can write the words and sentences here.

Lee and Pat
are with Mommy.

cannot

The cat cannot come
in the house. The
dog can come in the
house. The cat cannot.

You can write the words and sentences here.

children

Lee and Pat are good children. Mommy and daddy like good children.

All / all

You can write the words and sentences here.

All the children are here.

We / we

We can all go in the car. We like to go in the car.

You can write the words and sentences here.

Let's

Let's go in the car with Mommy and Daddy.

Come on!

You can write the words and sentences here.

Come on! Let's go!
Let's go over there.

Have / have

You can write the words and sentences here.

They have ice-creams over there. They have good ice-creams. We like ice-creams. We like all ice-creams.

Be / be

Daddy wants the children to be good. He likes good children.

You can write the words and sentences here.

Please / please

Please be good.
Be good children.
I like good children.

us

You can write the words and sentences here.

The dog can come
with us. He can
come in the car with us.
Kim is a very good dog.
We like Kim to come with us.

See / see

You can write the words and sentences here.

Lee and Pat
are here.

Lee can see the
ice-creams. Pat
can see the
ice-creams, too. The
ice-creams are very good.

You can write the words and sentences here.

The End

If the young reader can read and understand all the key words
and sentences above, he/she will now be able to independently
read and understand all the stories in
Word by Word Readers: Level 1 Collection.

This collection contains the first 3 books in the 12-book series.

See the book on Amazon at:
http://hyperurl.co/tfqnua

Happy Reading!

Made in the USA
Middletown, DE
07 May 2018